GW01458083

Visionary Leadership
in the Local Church

John Leach

Director of Anglican Renewal Ministries

GROVE BOOKS LIMITED

RIDLEY HALL RD CAMBRIDGE CB3 9HU

Contents

To Robert, with grateful thanks.

The Cover Illustration is by Peter Ashton

First Impression December 1997
ISSN 0144-171X
ISBN 1 85174 360 X

1
Introduction

This book will guarantee church growth! A modest claim, I know, but I am going to suggest a strategy which, if the church could find the will to adopt it, even in spite of its inherent difficulties, would mean that growth, health and vitality would become a way of life. I write as an Anglican, but I believe that this will work in any denomination. What is this radical strategy? You will have to wait until the end of the book; before we get to it I need to explain why it will work, and why it is so urgent that we consider it. The general subject is that of vision; the specific strategy comes later.

'Where there is no vision, the people perish.' The Authorised Version's translation of Proverbs 29.18 is, sadly, a pretty inaccurate one. The sense is much more about people running wild and letting their hair down in the absence of prophetic revelation to curb them. On most of the occasions on which I have heard this verse quoted in the context of vision it has been misused completely. However, in spite of that, the thesis of this booklet is that where there is no vision, the people perish. I believe that to be true, whether or not the Bible explicitly teaches it in that particular verse.

I believe that the single greatest lack in parish ministry currently is that of vision, and that this explains the unhealthy situation of much of the church. This booklet will attempt to define what I mean by the terms 'vision' and 'visionary leadership,' examine some of the symptoms of visionless churches and leadership, and begin an exploration of how we can become more visionary. After all that we will arrive at my radical strategy for the future.

I will not need to spend very much time arguing that the church is not in a good state—the statistics have done that far more eloquently. The hard fact is that we (perhaps especially those of us who are Anglicans) are in a church which is largely in the process of dying. There are small areas of hope, of course, but they seem to be having about as much effect on the overall picture as pouring a kettle of boiling water into Lake Windermere in an attempt to warm it up. The result is all but negligible.

Neither do I want to spend time arguing that the church ought to be healthy, growing and vibrant, since this too has been argued convincingly elsewhere. Church growth 'guru' Donald McGavran propounds a theology of a 'finding God' who is concerned with results since results are actually people reconciled to him and won to his kingdom.[1] Personally I find his

---

1   McGavran, D A, *Understanding Church Growth* (Grand Rapids, Michigan: Eerdmans, 1980) p 23ff.

arguments compelling, and cannot help but conclude that as the church in Britain we are not doing very well.

But what I do want to argue is that one of the major reasons for this malaise is the lack of vision among the churches' leadership. To put it simply, most of those in leadership at all levels within local churches have not yet caught or been taught the art of being visionary.

Neither is this purely about numerical growth. The quality of life of many churches leaves much to be desired; this I will explore in the next section, and I will argue that this too is a factor of visionless leadership.

So what is this thing called 'vision'? Jazz musician Duke Ellington, when asked to define 'rhythm,' replied 'If you got it, you don't need no definition. And if you don't have it, ain't no definition gonna help.'[2] The same may be said for vision, although I believe it can be learned, and attempts to define or explain it are useful. Jonathan Swift in the seventeenth century, for example, called it 'the art of seeing things invisible'; various church leaders have working definitions such as 'seeing the invisible and making it visible,' 'an informed bridge from the present to the future,' 'sanctified dreams' and 'a picture held in your mind's eye of the way things could or should be in the days ahead.' Christian researcher and consultant George Barna defines vision for ministry as 'a reflection of what God wants to accomplish through you to build his kingdom,'[3] and John Wimber spoke of 'writing your history in advance.'

For what they are worth, my working definitions—those which will form the basis of this book—are these:

Vision—the ability to see what could be rather than just what is.

Leaders—those who walk into the future, take a look around, and then return and tell the people to follow them back to the future or, more simply, —those whom God tells before he tells anyone else.

In other words, my belief is that the prime task of church leadership is to lead people into a future which is different from, and better than, the current state of affairs. Joshua exemplifies this clearly. He went in to spy out the Promised Land, returned to the people and told them that they could get there, in spite of the difficulties, and then became part of the team which led them there over the next thirty-eight years.

Once you accept that definition, it is easy to see how problems may arise if leaders are not doing this properly. Like the other ten spies they may have

---

2   Quoted in Barna, G. *The Power of Vision* (Ventura, CA: Regal, 1992) p 28.
3   *ibid*, p 28f.

vision squeezed out of them by the sheer weight of circumstances, or like the rest of the people they may simply not have seen anything of what lay ahead. They may feel happy, or at least stuck, with the status quo, and find it impossible to imagine anything different. When local churches have no vision, all sorts of symptoms may begin to show.

2
Where There is No Vision…

What might visionless church life look like? Here are some symptoms which may betray a lack of visionary leadership in the life of a local church.

Circularity

As a young deacon in my first curacy I was impressed by the splendid events which our somewhat anglo-catholic parish put on to celebrate occasions such as All Saints' Day, Advent Sunday, Carols by Candlelight, and so on. In particular I remember the 'Walk to Bethlehem,' a choral and liturgical extravaganza which marked with great beauty and impact the start of our Christmas celebrations. But the impact for me was lessened slightly the following year when exactly the same services were repeated *verbatim*, including all the same music. By my fourth year I was thoroughly sick of walking to Bethlehem, and would gladly have crawled to Bethnal Green just for the change. As far as I know they are still walking.

I did not know it at the time, but the church was functioning with a Greek philosophy of history, where life is an endless cycle repeating itself into eternity. This might be represented diagrammatically like this:

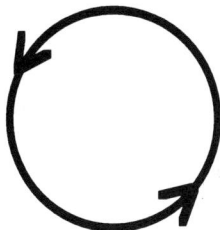

Some churches, on the other hand, function with a Hebrew understanding, which is much more linear. We are not going round in circles; we are going somewhere, and once we have been there we are never ever going there again! This view might look like this:

Perhaps a more helpful model than either of these two might look like this:

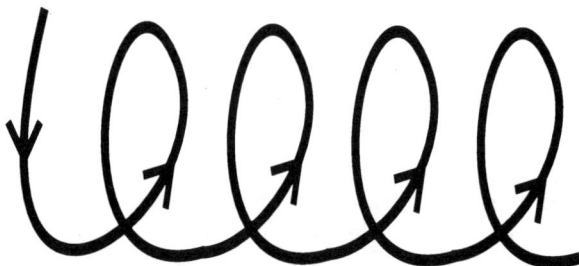

We do have an element of circularity, given to us for example by the church's year and liturgical calendar, but at the same time there is a sense of forward motion, of celebrating old occasions in new ways. A desire to escape from the circle of church life is, I believe, behind much of the discontent with the 1978 lectionary, which the Anglican church is in the process of replacing with the Revised Common Lectionary. No longer will we be preaching on the same themes again and again, but we will be much more free to ask the question 'What is the Spirit saying to the church through the text *now*, for this period of its life?' A similar trend may be seen in the growing interest in 'cell groups' rather than home groups, one characteristic of which is their sense of purpose: the declared aim is to reach the point of multiplication within a given time, not just to meet together studying Lent books until the Second Coming.

Fragmentation

Vision has a uniting effect on those who have bought into it. In the early years of my incumbency the PCC went through the trendy but nevertheless helpful process of writing a 'Vision Statement.' You know the sort of thing: complete the sentence 'This church exists to…' in less than fifty words. As is often the case, the process was far more useful than the end product, but one unexpected side-effect was the number of things we stopped doing. Since we now knew what we existed for, we were able to take a long, hard look at some of the things we were busy with, only to discover that we were not actually there to do them. Midweek services for two or three people, involvement in schools way outside the parish, groups or services which had outlived their usefulness—all these and many more things were gradually stopped. The energy we saved in not doing them could then be focused on doing more efficiently and effectively the things we were there to do.

Visionless churches are often loaded down with a multitude of activities and organizations which give the impression of busyness but are actually fragmenting the life of the church, with everyone doing what is right in their own eyes. An exciting vision, well communicated, can draw people together and help them to work as a team towards common ends.

Drivenness

Tied in with this is the church's expectation that it must do everything demanded of it. Another way of disposing of the liturgical calendar would be to respond positively to every single demand which drops through the letter box to celebrate this, that or the other 'Sunday.' Letters arrive in their droves, informing us that Sea Sunday, Education Sunday, Prison Sunday, Leprosy Sunday, Cruelty to Hamsters Sunday or whatever is coming up, and providing us with helpful sermon outlines, intercessions and suggested hymns. And that is just the Sundays! 'Your church should be involved with the elderly!' we are told. 'What are you doing about youth?' 'How are you ministering to the New Age travellers in your area?' 'What about HIV?' the strident voices cry, with the result that we are left wallowing in guilt, losing sight of what we have achieved in the welter of what we have not.

The discernment of a clear vision can help us to say a clear 'No.' Over the years I have gained great encouragement from Mark 1.35-38:

Very early in the morning, while it was still dark, Jesus got up, left the house and went off to a solitary place, where he prayed. Simon and his companions went to look for him, and when they found him, they exclaimed: 'Everyone is looking for you!'

Jesus replied, 'Let us go somewhere else—to the nearby villages—so that I can preach there also. That is why I have come.'

Facing the demands of others, Jesus has no problem whatsoever with saying 'No,' not because the demands are not valid, the needs urgent or the causes excellent, but simply because he has his own agenda, given to him by the Father, and he has the courage of his convictions to stick ruthlessly to it. Visionless churches have no such agenda, and are therefore at the mercy of anyone who turns up with a need which they want met. Life becomes hectic and driven, and guilt-ridden too, because there are always just too many demands to meet. Knowing what God has called you to do is a great help in knowing what he has not.

Empire-building

When this drivenness occurs, there is often a fragmentation as people pursue their own ideas and causes, and try to get everyone else to as well. Even within the 'internal' life of the church, different areas can grow up and compete for people's attention. There can often be an element of the personality cult which grows as some people who oversee different areas in the life of the church try to see their 'empire' expand. The most common area in which this may happen is that of music, but it is by no means the only one. People who gain their security from the status they have may find it hard to work towards a common vision and purpose where their contribution, whilst greatly valued, is not the only one!

This is particularly a problem within British church culture, which is largely characterized by being 'graceless.' Protestants are driven by the work ethic through which their status is measured by what they achieve, and Catholics are so often taught that 'faith is effort,' spirituality is hard work and pain is gain. Few Christians really and deeply know themselves to be accepted by God, and thus are constantly trying to earn his approval and demonstrate it to others.[4] The more this is a problem, the greater the degree of vision needed to capture the hearts of those who may find it difficult.

Listlessness

If these are symptoms of too much activity which is badly focused, the equal and opposite dangers are of a kind of listless inactivity in which no-one does very much at all. The church life struggles on, but without much interest or enthusiasm from the members. Since there is little sense of going anywhere, it really does not seem to be worth the bother of doing anything. Church becomes an hour on Sunday mornings; there is little sense of a faith lived out during the week.

Alongside this ennui may be a sense of despair. What is the point? We are going nowhere; nothing will ever change around here, so we will keep our heads down and live with the status quo, remembering the motto of many churches: 'As it was in the beginning, is now and ever shall be, world without end. Amen.'

Self-satisfaction

On the other hand, however, despair may not enter into things at all. Another symptom of a lack of vision is a sense of pride and comfort. We may

---

4 In my experience those involved in Freemasonry are especially prone to this temptation to empire-building. My theory is that an organization which quite deliberately preaches salvation by works, and which has as its highest value promotion up the hierarchy to a position of greater honour, makes Christian servanthood and humility extremely difficult virtues to develop among its members.

not have arrived, but we have come a long way. A market-town church I know usually attracted about 200 people on a Sunday morning. When compared with the churches in the villages around where the attendance rarely broke into double figures, this seemed like tremendous success. So it was easy to settle back, forgetting the fact that the village churches probably had a much larger proportion of the population at worship than they did, and tiptoeing by the 8,800 people in the town they had yet to reach. It is salutary to hear an African pastor bewailing his failure because of the 300 people in his village there are still ten who do not attend church!

If a church does look busy and successful, particularly in comparison to others, it may seem to be the case that everything in the garden is rosy. Any suggestion that things might be done in a different way is heard as a denial of the value of that which is being done, and to be told that there might be room for improvement feels like a slap in the face or a pin in the balloon, and is therefore rejected summarily.

Poor Quality

One of the values which seems to be present in healthy and growing churches is that of quality. In other words, they try to do everything they do as well as they can. So if the weekly notice-sheet comes out of the photo-copier with black blotches all over it, they bin it and do it again properly. They replace grubby and tatty vestments, ask musicians to rehearse, serve pleasant-tasting as well as politically correct coffee, remove notices the morning after the event which they publicized is over, and so on. These little touches tell people that they feel that what they are trying to do is important enough to do well, and that the God for whom they are doing it deserves only the best.

Visionless churches have little interest in quality, and little concern for public image. Any old slapdash thing will do, since there is so little at stake other than keeping doing what they have always been doing. 'Make-do-and-mend' is the church motto, sometimes even without the 'mend' bit.

Money Problems

Yes, every church does have them, but a low level of financial commitment may be a symptom of a deeper malaise, the belief (often unarticulated) that there is nothing here really worth giving to. Robert Warren tells the story of the Church Extension Project at St Thomas' Crookes in Sheffield, and the incredible financial sacrifices which people made for the huge vision which had been set before them.[5] Reflecting on this experience, he states the truth that 'People will make great sacrifices once they see what they are

5   Warren, R. *In the Crucible* (Crowborough: Highland, 1989) p 85ff.

being called to make sacrifices for, and are convinced of the worth of what is being done.'[6] Many other stories of incredible sacrifice abound, from a whole variety of different church contexts.

The corollary is that a lack of sacrificial giving may indicate that nothing is being asked of people which will stretch them and challenge their allegiance to the god of money. And of course this is true not just of money but also of their giving of time, skills and effort.

Ideas, Not Visions

Many churches, of course, do not carry on oblivious to these sorts of issues or behaviour patterns. On the contrary, they know things are not as they should be, and that there is room for improvement. Something needs to happen, so the search begins for Ideas. 'We could buy a new keyboard!' exclaims one church council member. 'How about a youth group?' asks another. 'St Kevin's down the road do *Alpha*,' says a third. 'Why don't we?' And so it goes on—all sorts of good ideas but no overriding vision, no questions about whether *Alpha* is right for us now, or whether God really is calling us to youth work when the average age of the parish inhabitants is fifty three. Neither is there any sense of timing. Maybe we should be thinking about a particular course of action, but is now really the right time? An overriding vision and purpose would allow each of these ideas to be carefully assessed to see whether or not it contributed appropriately to the bigger picture. But a collection of good ideas is just that—it is neither a vision nor a strategy.

Does any of this feel familiar? This may have been a painful section to read, and it is not, of course, my desire to produce guilt or to de-skill people. But we are all too accomplished in the church at playing 'Let us pretend.' Haggai stood looking at the ruins of the Temple and asked the people one of the most important questions anyone can ever ask 'How does it look to you now?' (Haggai 2.3) Had the people answered 'Not too bad, when you compare it with the Temple down the road in the next parish' they would never have found the motivation to begin the hard work of rebuilding. Until we have heard and received the bad news, even if it sends us almost to rock bottom, we will never feel the need for the good. And there is good news. These symptoms come from a malaise which can be cured. So how can churches and their leaders become visionary?

6   *ibid*, p 93f

3
Vision, Leadership and Authority

Before we attempt to answer that question we need to define some terms more carefully. Just whose job is it to be visionary? What is the relationship between vision and leadership? In the first section we mentioned Joshua. He functioned in the example we looked at as a visionary, but he was not (at least for the next few decades) the leader of the people. Whose job is it to lead a local church, and whose job is it to be the visionary?

In many cases the leader is the visionary. He or she senses from God what the direction is to be, and then leads the people in that way. This is not always the case, however. If you are a leader but do not feel particularly visionary, all is not lost!

There is an increasing emphasis in the church currently on leadership teams and collaborative ministry. This is clearly something to be welcomed, not least because it removes the pressure from the clergy or professional leadership to be omnicompetent. More and more church leaders are finding great release in working with a team, and it may be the case that it is one of the team rather than the overall leader who is the most visionary. However, the leader still has considerable power, not least because of the authority which goes with the job. What this means is that whilst the leader may not be the person who usually originates the vision, he or she has the power to stop it in its tracks, simply by not leading people into it. Thus the leader who is not visionary needs to be able convincingly to communicate the visions of others (which have hopefully become the visions of the whole team). I will say more about the authority of leadership later on, but for now let me suggest that the biblical model of the relationship between the prophet and the king is a helpful one in understanding this dynamic. The prophet would often bring God's word to the king, but from then on it was left rather at his royal mercy. He could choose to let it die simply by refusing to communicate or act upon it, or he could lead the nation in the direction given to him by the prophet. I want to allow for lots of different models of leadership in the local church, and for the contribution of lots of different people into it, but at the end of the day I believe that one overall leader has the authority either to make the vision happen or not.

4
Becoming Visionary

So how can we learn to become more visionary? The first step towards visionary leadership is to understand that the church is God's, not ours. During the 1980s one message began to emerge from several different sources: 'God wants his church back.' He has a purpose for the church, and for each individual congregation within it, and he wants to be allowed to work it out and make it happen as he wants—to lead us into the inheritance it has always been his purpose to give us. The task of leadership is therefore one of discovery rather than invention. We do not have the incredible burden of thinking up what to do next; the key is to learn to hear God's voice and follow his agenda.

This is such good news for anyone in church leadership; God knows what he is doing, and he wants to communicate his strategy to us, as well as leading us along the way.

This does presuppose, of course, that we have first corrected an inherited misunderstanding about the nature of church. We need to see it as a dynamic rather than a static entity. The biblical pictures of pilgrimage are helpful here; God's people were so often on a journey. Even when it was not a physical, geographical journey there was still a sense of spiritual forward motion and purpose. A classic text, though, does describe a physical journey—that from Egypt to the Promised Land.

That journey had existed in the mind of God from eternity. The first to hear about it was Abraham, to whom God revealed the vision of a great nation living in a land which he himself would give them, a land which significantly became known as the 'Promised Land.' Centuries later Moses was given a glimpse of that vision, as he was called to be the leader who would take the people on the next phase of their journey:

> The LORD said, 'I have indeed seen the misery of my people in Egypt. I have heard them crying out because of their slave drivers, and I am concerned about their suffering. So I have come down to rescue them from the hand of the Egyptians and to bring them up out of that land into a good and spacious land, a land flowing with milk and honey—the home of the Canaanites, Hittites, Amorites, Perizzites, Hivites and Jebusites.'
> (Exodus 3.7-8)

It was not up to Moses to decide where to take the people once he had rescued them from slavery; God already had a plan, and its final conclusion was very specific—you could actually find the destination on a map. But if the general outline was in place, what of the fine detail? Again, God was there to lead and guide:

By day the LORD went ahead of them in a pillar of cloud to guide them on their way and by night in a pillar of fire to give them light, so that they could travel by day or night. Neither the pillar of cloud by day nor the pillar of fire by night left its place in front of the people. (Ex 13.21-22)

A later portion of the narrative explains this more fully. Whenever the cloud lifted from above the Tent, the Israelites set out; wherever it settled, they encamped. As long as it stayed over the tabernacle, they remained in camp. Sometimes it was over the tabernacle only a few days; sometimes it stayed only from evening till morning. But whether it stayed over the tabernacle for two days or a month or a year, the Israelites would remain in camp and not set out; but when it lifted, they would set out (Num 9.17-23). That's what you call detail!

The 'journey' of the gospel from Jerusalem, through Judea and Samaria to the ends of the earth is another example of God's strategy being revealed to his leaders. On a first reading the book of Acts can seem quite haphazard, but from the vantage point of the end of the story it is clear that there has been a strategy, and that the apostles have responded along the way to the guidance of God as he has revealed his will and purpose to them in a variety of ways. Sometimes this was through an active call *to* somewhere, sometimes through prevention *from* going somewhere, sometimes through what at the time must have looked purely like 'circumstances' but which in retrospect we can see was the providence of God. Sometimes the supernatural power of the Holy Spirit broke in messily, causing everyone to rethink that which they had always taken for granted; sometimes there is the sense that God's best purposes had been thwarted by human intransigence, causing the apostles to obey Jesus' command to give up, shake the dust from their feet and go elsewhere where there was greater openness.[7] And at times human (but hopefully sanctified) common sense seemed to dictate that a certain course of action seemed to be appropriate.

Why then should leaders think that the journey they are called to lead their churches on should be of their own devising? Surely the God who was quite capable of leading his people in the past can still speak today to those of us called to be leaders. It is not, of course, as easy as it appeared to be in the days of the Bible. It would be great if a pillar of fire appeared at our Church Council meetings with a casting vote, or the odd angel turned up at

---

7   A policy, interestingly, which the Anglican Church has steadfastly refused to follow!

Deanery Synod. But I suspect that our lack of clear divine guidance is often more to do with our inability to hear than God's to speak.

We begin to become visionary, then, when we grasp the truth that we are on a journey, and that God is with us both as guide and companion. He has a plan, a route and a strategy for us, and our task as leaders or leadership teams is to discern that strategy and to convince others to walk with him in it.

Dreams and Visions

This then opens up all sorts of new possibilities. Knowing that God is in control sets us free from the anxiety of having to conjure up our own plans for where we would like to go. But at the same time, and quite paradoxically, it sets us free to dream dreams. Just where might we be going with God? Could it be that his plan for us is to grow to a membership of four thousand, or even more? Or might we hear his call to plant fifteen different congregations within the patch? Could we see the parents from our church so influence the local school that kingdom values might be in evidence throughout its life? Might we see those who work for the city council being promoted to key positions because they were renowned for their honesty and integrity? Could it be our church to whom God gives a ministry of healing to those with the AIDS virus? Might the population in our village, like some villages in other parts of the world, be ninety-per-cent Spirit-filled Christians? When God is in charge, the possibilities are endless. In order to grasp what God's specific purpose for us is, we first need to expand our minds so that they can even conceive of the kind of scale he might be working on. His purposes might be quite modest, in fact; we must not fall into the world's trap of thinking that big is necessarily beautiful. But that said, his plans are probably less modest than we think, and are so often limited by what we believe possible.

This kind of 'possibility-thinking' is an important step in becoming visionary, and it is a kind of body-building exercise which can toughen us up and help us run with the specific vision of God for us once we have picked it up. Martin Luther King had a dream which must have seemed no more than a pipe-dream to many of those who heard him speak of it, yet it captured the imagination of a generation and began the process of liberation which still continues today. Where congregations are small and dispirited, and where the social factors combine to give messages which tell us that we can achieve absolutely nothing, there is nothing more empowering to us than having a leader tell us that we have a God who is capable of anything. Congregations which have had any kind of personal hope or vision knocked out of them long since by the sheer reality of the grind of life can begin to see God's possibilities if helped to do so by a faith-filled visionary leader. We can learn again what it means to think ambitious thoughts with him.

14

Getting the Picture

So how do we grasp God's vision? So far we have tried to ensure that our minds are big enough to contain it, and in our wildest moments of abandon we have some impossible dreams up our sleeves. In my experience there are two dimensions to vision, which have both been illustrated in the story of the journey to the Promised Land.

The first is the big picture: where is God taking us long-term? We know the final destination, of course, but before that what are we to become? A useful question to ask (of ourselves and of God) is 'What could this church be like in thirty years' time?' How large might it be? What special areas of outreach or ministry might God have given us? What could our influence be on the city/town/village's social and political life? What does God plan to use us to achieve in the schools/university around us? Part of the answers to these questions will lie in the realm of our dreams and hopes, but as we dream something may really catch fire for us, grabbing our attention and becoming all-consuming. This is the equivalent of the 'Promised Land' dimension, describing where we might end up long-term.

But the other dimension is the cloud-and-fire, nuts-and-bolts day-by-day direction of the church. How do we seek God's will in the many decisions which we have to make almost daily? Having the long-term vision clearly in view first is essential in assessing the more short-term direction. The first question to ask is 'Will this particular course of action take us in the direction we are wanting to go in?' If it contradicts, or seems to veer us away from the long-term aim, it might not be right for us now. This is not foolproof, of course. To trace on a map the journey from Goshen to Canaan shows that God does not always travel as the crow flies! But nevertheless we will want to ensure that most of the time the details seem to fit with the overall picture.

So how do we hear God? Visionary ideas are most commonly given to individuals to be checked out by a team. To expect a committee to be creative is to be hopeful indeed. Vision comes to individuals, sometimes out of the blue but most often as they are still, on their knees or their faces, before God. They tend sometimes to come to people at rock bottom: usually it is only when our plans have all come to nothing that we are desperate enough to listen for his.

When vision comes to an individual it will be mediated through his or her personality. We naturally expect everyone to be the same as we are, and to function in the same ways (ask any marriage counsellor about that!). The gurus of the Myers-Briggs Type Indicator (an attempt to help us understand ourselves which many Christians have found tremendously useful) tell us that we all feel more comfortable working in some ways than others. Some of us are primarily thinkers who enjoy theories and principles whilst others are far more interested in real people and situations, and some of us analyse information gathered through our five senses while others often make use of a 'sixth sense,' intuition, or feeling of 'rightness.' Vision is unlikely to by-pass these natural tendencies within us, and we can learn to recognize and relax into them. As a strong intuitive I often 'just feel' that a particular course of action is the right one. My more analytical friends want data and information to back up this decision, and I simply do not have any. I just have a feeling. It has taken me many years to learn to trust this intuition as a God-given gift through which he speaks to me in ways I can comfortably hear. The 'hard' evidence often comes later, once we have taken the risk of going with my hunch. Most times it has worked out! Other leaders will be much more at home with facts rather than feelings, and will understand God's purposes through graphs, charts and statistics.

Dreams are Made of This

What are the raw materials of vision? Sometimes vision for a particular situation will come from something we have seen in real life somewhere else. The music ministry in my last parish grew to be based heavily on a model we saw each year at Spring Harvest. I had arrived to find a sole diet of robed choir and organ, but could see in my mind's eye a blend of traditional and modern music with a band alongside the organ. This vision took a couple of years to realize, but by then I had seen something even better, and off we went again.

Sometimes vision will come directly from the pages of Scripture. The video *Viva Christo Rey!* tells the story of a church given a vision for caring for the people who lived and worked on the rubbish tips on the Texas/Mexico border. This came out of a reading of Luke 14.12-14,

'When you give a luncheon or dinner, do not invite your friends, your brothers or relatives, or your rich neighbours; if you do, they may invite you back and so you will be repaid. But when you give a banquet, invite the poor, the crippled, the lame, the blind, and you will be blessed. Although they cannot repay you, you will be repaid at the resurrection of the righteous.'

They were convicted as they read those words to take them literally and obey them. As they went they saw a miraculous multiplication of food, and eventually a great harvest for the kingdom.

Sometimes vision will come through what the Americans call 'hanging out'—simply being with others and bouncing ideas around. Most of the good things that happen at Church Council meetings happen during the coffee break or in the pub afterwards, away from the pressure of agendas, minutes and decisions. Even those who seem bereft of any vision at all can begin to blossom in the right surroundings! A wise leadership team will build in plenty of time just to be together; it may turn out to be the most valuable time of all.

Very often, in my experience, vision comes in the context of worship. Many churches have been learning much recently about the call to intimacy with God, so that worship becomes less of a dull routine or a route-march through the words in the book, but a time to draw closer to God. In such times of intimacy we can sometimes hear the inspiring whisperings of his voice. I heard someone say once that they had 'had an idea whilst I was praying,' this seems to me to be the essence of hearing God through worship. God's word might come through a direct prophetic or revelatory word, or through a sense deep within the spirit, but new direction has often come out of the most intimate of worship sessions.

Dreams (the kind that happen while you are asleep) also have a good biblical track record for revealing God's will. Our rational mindset and society mean that we seldom consider such non-rational (but not irrational) means of revelation, but the Bible speaks of many situations where dreams are highly significant. My wife Chris' ministry with children, and her subsequent writing on the subject, were brought to a significant new level through a powerful dream.[8] And of course we must not forget the role played in the biblical narratives by angels, theophanies and audible voices. Whilst I have not got any personal stories to tell you about any of those, to my shame, I do know of one curate who heard God speak audibly about his future ministry during a rather dull staff meeting. Also, there are in print today all sorts of accounts of visitations by angels. I see no reason to believe that God ever stopped using these methods of communication; it is a shame they are as rare as they seem to be.

Once the individual has some kind of an impression for the way forward, the rest of the leadership team come into their own, bringing their complementary gifts and personalities to bear. The visionary 'feeler' is not allowed to get away with an infallible 'that is what I just felt we should do' as the others lovingly and prayerfully go about their business on the idea. It may seem like a good idea, but can it actually work, even with the grace of God? The principle sounds great, but what will it do to the people involved? Vision is thrashed out, not by those committed to being wet blankets, but by other visionaries who might just hear God in different ways.

Selling the Vision

Having prayed and talked through the vision, the next role of the leader, whether or not the vision originally came from him or her, is to communicate or 'cast' it to the rest of the church. An important principle comes into

---

8   See Russ Parker's Grove booklet S 15 *Dreams and Spirituality.*

play here, which we have already mentioned. It may be controversial, but I will say it anyway, since I believe it to be true: leaders have the right to lead. If you, as the leader of a congregation, have arrived at a God-given vision of what he wants to do with them, you also have the God-given authority to tell them so and to help them to follow him.

I think we have become frightened of this. There have been so many situations in the past where a priestly caste has ruled the church with a rod of iron, often simply to feather its own nest, or where a charismatic individual has used his leadership to manipulate or oppress others. The whole politically-correct spirit of the age has militated against leadership, as has leadership itself with increasing revelations of corruption and sleaze. We live in times which are strictly anti-authority, and democracy and empowerment are the buzz-words of the new millennium.

I wonder, however, whether the church has jumped too readily onto this bandwagon, and whether the answer to bad leadership is not no leadership but proper leadership. Given the servant-leadership shown and taught by Jesus himself, which seems to me to be a non-negotiable factor in any Christian leadership, there are still many different models, even within the pages of the Bible. But I am not convinced that pure democracy is one of them. It sounds like a good idea, but it is not to be confused with being a Christian idea. Moses did not hold a referendum on whether or not the people should return to slavery. In a 'heavy' 'paternalistic' way he told them to stop grizzling and get going. He and God knew what was good for them. He had received a vision of the ultimate destination and was so committed to getting them there that he would not be diverted by their ignorance and immaturity.

But is not this 'parental,' 'controlling' and 'de-skilling'? Did it not breed an unhealthy dependence on Moses? And did it not generate in him a 'Messiah complex'? Not a bit of it—it was a mark of his love and care for the people that he steadfastly led them beyond their moaning into the joy awaiting them. We see him happy to work in a team with Aaron and later Joshua, we see him delegating authority and building a highly effective management structure (for which the original vision had come from someone else, whilst he was struggling and defeated), and we see him longing that more of the people could be filled with the Spirit and function prophetically.

I believe that the church has lost its nerve to a high degree over leadership. I was told quite clearly at college in the late 70s that there was no such thing in the Bible! A whole generation of clergy have been trained out of leadership rather than into it, (although fortunately many have been able to rediscover it), while people in congregations across the land are left feeling the tragic lack of it. People want to be led, and they want people they love and trust to do it. Those placed in charge of local churches do well to look again at what the Bible has to say about leadership, as well as learning from

18

those bringing secular expertise to bear on church leadership.[9]

So if someone has a sense of where God might be taking you, and a group of leaders have prayerfully arrived at the place of agreement, the overall leader has the right to communicate that vision to the church. Preaching, teaching, writing and discussion will be helpful media for this communication, and the style should be more like 'This is where we think God is taking us' than 'Does anyone have any idea where God might be taking us?' or even 'What do you mean "taking us?"' The task of managing the change may not be an easy one, and much wisdom will be needed, but the task must be undertaken with courage and steadfastness if that which God has graciously shown us is to be worked out.

Vision and Timing

'Seal up the vision, for it concerns the distant future' said the angel to Daniel. Discerning God's timing is crucial in visionary leadership. Daniel was so overwhelmed by what he saw that he

...was exhausted and lay ill for several days. Then I got up and went about the king's business. I was appalled by the vision; it was beyond understanding. (Daniel 8.27)

A similar reaction can occur if we try to communicate our vision before the general public are ready to receive it! The vision we see of the future may be unpalatable or indigestible to everyone else at the moment. Or it may simply not be 'ripe' yet. Nehemiah was given a burden for the state of the city of Jerusalem whilst in exile, but it was four months (from Kislev to Nisan) before he was given the opportunity to ask the king if he might return and rebuild. He might well have blown the whole thing had he been overwhelmed by the strength of the vision but lacked the patience to wait for God's timing. Visions often need to be marinaded in prayer before they are ready.

Sometimes there is preliminary work to be done in creating a little discontent. When I was first shown into the church building during my interview for the post of vicar, I decided within about two seconds where the OHP screen would go (it is a well known fact that revival will never come to a church without an OHP screen!). But to have told the Wardens at the interview that I wanted to mutilate their beautiful building with a large screen would have been a suicidal career move. So I sealed up the vision until a more opportune time.

When we did eventually begin to use projected songs in our worship (and that is another story), we shone the words straight onto the grey stone

---

9   For what it is worth, my favourite leadership books are Tom Marshall *Understanding Leadership* (Chichester: Sovereign World, 1991), James Dunn *The Effective Leader* (Eastbourne: Kingsway, 1995) and John Harvey Jones *Making it Happen* (London: Fontana, 1989).

wall. There was, as you might expect, a certain amount of opposition to this, but it was not because we were singing inane charismatic choruses. It was because people could not read the words of the inane charismatic choruses against the grey wall. It was only a matter of time before someone suggested that a screen screwed to the wall might help, a suggestion which was received with grateful acclaim by both the congregation and the vicar! God's words to Habbakuk need to be heard by every frustrated visionary:

The revelation awaits an appointed time;
it speaks of the end and will not prove false.
Though it linger, wait for it;
it will certainly come and will not delay.   (Habbakuk 2.3)

Who is This Dreamer?

As leaders we need to understand that much of our journey will be neutral as far as God is concerned, and will be up to us. God may have both grand and detailed plans for us, but the colour of the teacups in the church hall may not feature significantly in them. Like a loving father he will at times say to us 'What do you feel like doing?' and like a father he will allow us to develop a personality of our own as we make our own choices.

Knowing who we are as a church is important in the communal grasping of vision. As well as writing our vision statement, we found it helpful as a church to articulate our values, a list of seven things which helped, by describing what was important to us, define our church's 'personality.' We recognized the fact that much of our corporate personality would reflect that of the vicar, whilst ensuring that it did not do so exclusively. We were, for example, an Anglican church and proud of it! We did not believe that in order to grow we had to abandon liturgy and ceremonial and behave as if we were a Vineyard fellowship. So we worked hard at doing our liturgy with the quality which another of our values described, and of allowing within it the freedom for the Spirit to move which our value of being a supernatural church demanded. These and the other values were articulated frequently in magazines and bulletins, and they became almost like catchphrases around the church: when someone did spot a glaring typo on the notice-sheet or a large patch of mould in the kitchen the immediate response was to say with a wry smile 'We are a quality church!' Understanding its personality can help a church to know who it is, and therefore have a much clearer picture of who it might be in the glorious purposes of God.

Going for Gold

The final task of visionary leaders is to stick steadfastly to their guns and keep going for gold. There will be so many voices raised against a course of action, and so many diversionary tactics by the Enemy. Not all of them will come directly from the Enemy either. Jesus, having set his face steadfastly to go to Jerusalem to his death, hears the well-meaning protestations of one of his best friends, and yet discerns behind them the intentions of Satan to nudge him down a less demanding road (Matt 16.21–23).

Great discernment is needed to distinguish between those times when Satan is trying to divert us from the vision and those when circumstances dictate its adaptation. It is sadly possible for a leader to stick doggedly to a course of action which may have been fine ten years ago, but which is now in urgent need of an overhaul. It is not a case of seeking from God a once-for-all vision and never diverting from it by an inch; it is much more about walking day by day with him and seeking his guidance continually. But as a general guide, suspect enemy diversion whenever an easier path is suggested. Whilst training home group leaders I defined the leader's role as 'helping people down the more difficult path.' There is a kind of entropy by which people drift back towards the comfort zone. For the Israelites it was cucumbers, melons, leeks, onions and garlic which seemed so much more tempting than manna but which nearly robbed them of milk and honey. In the church too there are many more comfortable options which will eventually lead to slavery and death. The leader has to cast, recast and cast again the vision, constantly calling people back to it where they have drifted away in less demanding directions.

Does all this sound a tall order? If so, remember that at the end of the day people will respond to clear leadership and may even one day thank you for it. I remember visiting a town-centre church which had just completed a major reordering scheme only to be plunged into an interregnum. I got talking to a lady from the congregation who was there to help visitors and tourists, and after extolling the virtues of the previous vicar[10] she began to muse about his as yet unidentified successor. 'Whoever he turns out to be' she told me, 'I hope he really demands a lot from us!' Not what you would expect to hear perhaps, but her comment spoke volumes to me about what people really want from their leaders. Confidently to hold out a massive challenge to people and to tell them that with the grace of God we can get there is a profoundly attractive thing.

There is one final spin-off which is worth noting: visionary churches breed visionary church members. People carry out from the church into their 'secular' lives the idea that God does have a purpose which he is more than capable of fulfilling, and apply that principle to other areas of their lives. The church is not just the repository of vision, but a training ground for visionaries in other walks of life.

---

10 She was not the only one who appreciated him: he is now Archbishop of Canterbury!

5
A Radical Vision

At long last, here comes that strategy! Since it seems to be the case that vision produces vitality, mission and growth, a church which claims to take growth seriously must take vision seriously too, and must do all it can to ensure that it has a constant supply of visionary leaders. Let me illustrate how I think this would be possible, using own story.

My first curacy was spent in a Norfolk market town, and it was there I learnt the basics of pastoral parish ministry—hospital chaplaincy, a spell on a RAF station, lots of funerals, weddings and baptisms, regular home communions, and so on. This wide-ranging ministry taught me much which was essential, but it was not until I was fortunate enough to find a second curacy in a large Sheffield church that I really began to learn. The privilege of working alongside Robert Warren was so formative for me that I can scarcely express what a difference it made. Robert was the visionary *par excellence*, who constantly refused to be daunted by obstacles in the way of continual church growth. I learnt from him that problems were only there to be solved, and that they could be solved if only one kept nagging away at them for long enough. Whenever there was temptation to pull the vision down until it was easily within reach or shrink it to a more manageable size, he would flatly refuse to do so. He saw no reason why the church could not grow constantly, and life was therefore all about helping that to happen. His vision was not to fill the church with believers but to empty the parish of unbelievers, and his single-minded pursuit of this vision focused his energy and gave shape to all he did. I also learnt that large churches are not magic, unattainable places ruled over by the famous. We had our share of problems, many of them looking remarkably similar to those in rural Norfolk. Neither are they created overnight; a megachurch is just a small church which has been growing for a very long time.

So when I went to interview for my first incumbency I told the Parish Representatives with what must have seemed like incredible arrogance 'If I come here, we will grow.' It was not meant to be arrogant, it was just that I had caught something of Robert's way of thinking, and believed firmly that any church could grow eventually if it wanted to. There was nothing magic about St Thomas' Crookes: it just had a determined and visionary leader. I saw no reason why the lessons I had learnt could not be transferred to another parish, and no reason why my new church could not eventually grow to a membership of thousands. And grow we did. When I left the average Sunday throughput was 50% up on that at the start of my ministry, and I have every confidence that, given the right next incumbent, they should keep on growing.

The simple fact is that what I had learnt in that highly formative curacy was then transferred to my incumbency. This always tends to happen, of course, but what I had learnt particularly was the power of vision.

My story is not an isolated example. Without having done extensive research I am certain that growing churches tend to be led by leaders who have served as assistants to visionary leaders in growing churches. I could cite dozens of examples of healthy churches which are being led by those trained under visionaries; many other curates who worked with Robert Warren, for example, have gone on to lead churches into growth, and the same is true in several other situations. This can seem at times like rather threatening empire-building, but the hard facts suggest that those trained under gifted and successful visionary leaders will tend to go on and achieve great things for God in their own incumbencies.

The implications for this are painfully clear. If we are serious about church growth and vitality we must first begin to look during our selection procedures for those who have the potential to be visionary leaders, and then, I believe, as a specific and deliberate policy, we must begin to deploy assistant staff only alongside those who will train and infect them into visionary leadership.

Different dioceses will vary in their definitions of 'training parishes.' Some will be looking for somewhere which will provide the all-round basics which my first curacy gave me, whilst others will deliberately place assistant staff with those who may be struggling and need the support of working within a team. But it is my conviction that the single greatest thing we can do to ensure church growth in future generations is deliberately to build in vision to those who are in training by placing them with bosses who have a proven track record of church growth. The policy of placing curates in situations of safe mediocrity, or of (ab)using them to prop up dispirited incumbents in depressed situations does neither service to them for their future ministries nor to the church's ministry as a whole.

Consider the alternative. If new clergy are not being infected with a visionary streak which will remain with them, hopefully, throughout their lives, with what are they being infected? To begin ministry in a situation of maintenance rather than mission, of despair instead of hope, of low expectations rather than godly excitement is bound to have an effect on their future ministry. I would want to argue strongly that as a church we must grasp this nettle and begin a quite deliberate programme of investing in church growth leadership for the future.

There is also the question of ongoing support once curates become incumbents. Some Anglican dioceses are beginning to experiment with mentoring schemes, and this is to be welcomed on two conditions: it must be compulsory, since those who are most in need of help can be those who refuse to take it; and those acting as mentors must again be those with proven track records of growth and success. But the key principle is that vision can be taught and caught, and that we must invest in the future of the church by ensuring that our leaders are in situations where they can learn and catch it.

There will, of course, be many objections to such a radical strategy, and I have not the space here to forestall and argue against them. But where there is a will there is a way, and if we really are serious about wanting numerical and qualitative growth in the church we must first find the will, in spite of the obvious difficulties. We need to research churches which are actually growing, and their leaders. I am certain such research would demonstrate that there is a link between present growth and previous curacies. We would also need to begin cutting some losses and shaking off some dust in ruthless pursuit of this new policy. It will take time to make a difference, but I am convinced that in the long term we will begin to see the positive effects of such a policy in hope and growth.